Story-Picture Book

Level K

Lessons 81–112

A Division of The McGraw-Hill Companies

Columbus, Ohio

Illustration Credits

Dave Blanchette, Mark Corcoran, Susan DeMarco, John Edwards and Associates, Kersti Frigell, Simon Galkin, Meryl Henderson, Susan Jerde, Loretta Lustig, Steve McComber, Pat Schories, James Shough, Lauren Simeone, Rachel Taylor, and Gary Undercuffler.

www.sra4kids.com

SRA/McGraw-Hill

A Division of The **McGraw·Hill** Companies

Copyright © 2002 by SRA/McGraw-Hill.

Send all inquiries to:
SRA/McGraw-Hill
8787 Orion Place
Columbus, OH 43240-4027

Printed in the United States of America.

ISBN 0-07-568989-8

8 9 VHJ 06

Table of Contents

Peony
Pink

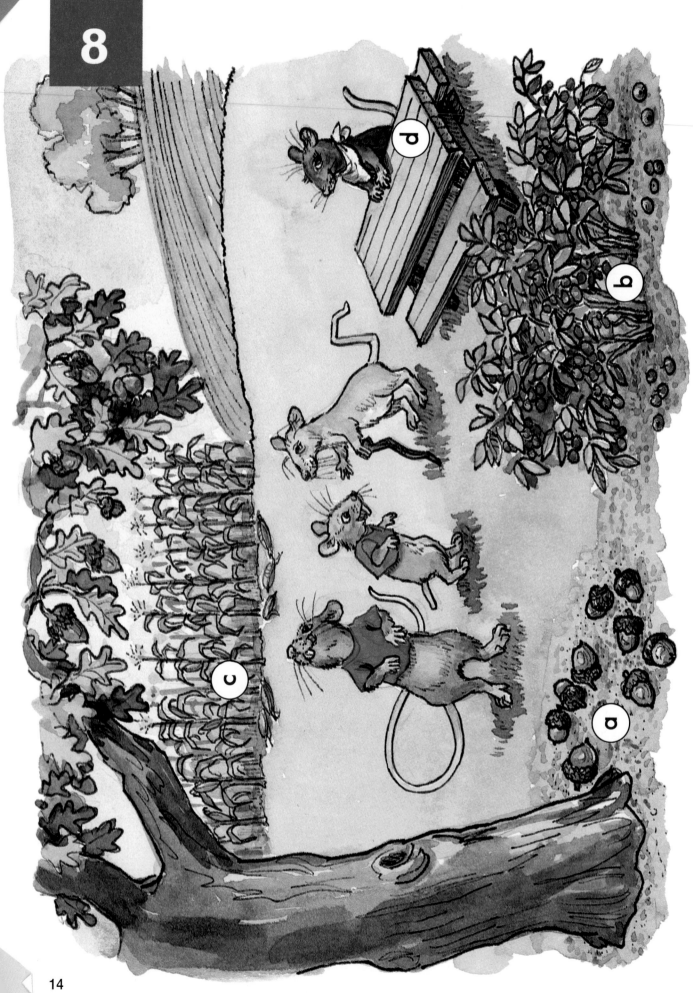

17

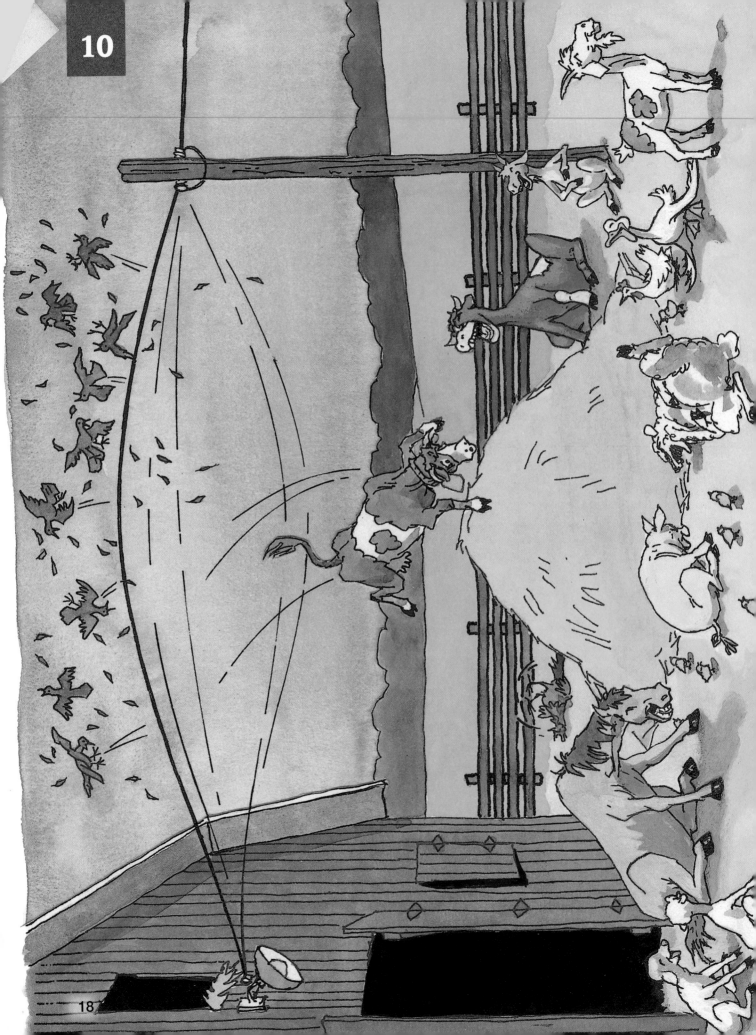

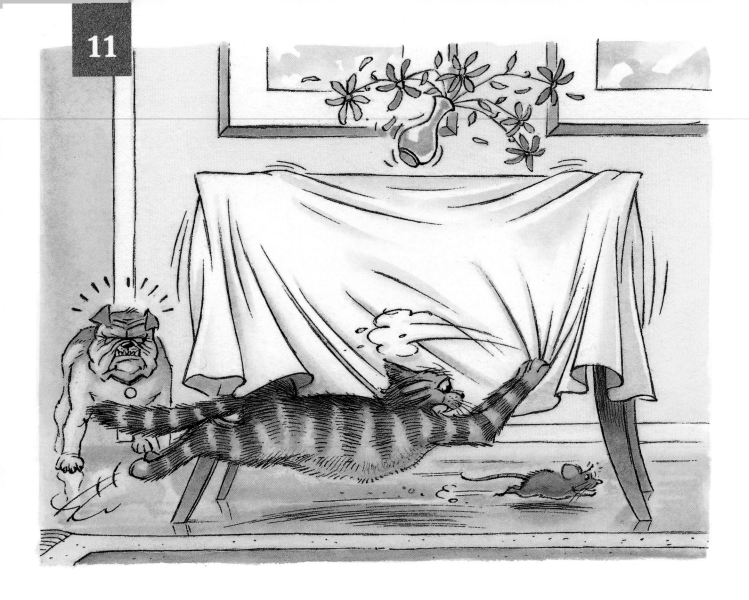